EDGE BOOKS

BEHIND THE SCENES WITH THE PROS

BEHIND THE SCENES OF PRO BASEBALL

BY CATHERINE ANN VELASCO

CAPSTONE PRESS
a capstone imprint

Edge Books are published by Capstone Press,
1710 Roe Crest Drive, North Mankato, Minnesota 56003
www.mycapstone.com

Library of Congress Cataloging-in-Publication Data
Names: Velasco, Catherine Ann, author.
Title: Behind the scenes of pro baseball / by Catherine Ann Velasco.
Description: North Mankato, Minnesota : Capstone Press, [2019] | Series: Behind the scenes with the pros | Includes bibliographical references and index. | Audience: Age 8-14. | Audience: Grade 7 to 8.
Identifiers: LCCN 2018043407 (print) | LCCN 2018053992 (ebook) | ISBN 9781543554328 (ebook) | ISBN 9781543554274 (hardcover : alk. paper) | ISBN 9781543559217 (pbk.)
Subjects: LCSH: Baseball--Training--Juvenile literature. | Baseball players--Health and hygiene--Juvenile literature. | Baseball players--Conduct of life--Juvenile literature. | Baseball players--Charitable contributions--Juvenile literature. | Baseball players--Salaries, etc.--Juvenile literature. | Major League Baseball (Organization)--Juvenile literature.
Classification: LCC GV867.5 (ebook) | LCC GV867.5 .V45 2019 (print) | DDC 796.357/64--dc23
LC record available at https://lccn.loc.gov/2018043407

Editorial Credits
Bradley Cole, editor; Craig Hinton, designer; Ryan Gale, production specialist

Photo Credits
Alamy: WorldFoto, 19; AP Images: Marcio Jose Sanchez, 11, Mark Duncan, cover; Icon Sportswire: Anthony J. Causi, 29, Mark LoMoglio, 7, Nick Wosika, 21, Tim Spyers, 25; Newscom: Bill Greenblatt/UPI, 23, David Berding/Icon Sportswire DFY, 27, Mike Theiler/Reuters, 8; Rex Features: Peter Joneleit/CSM, 5, Shawn Thew/Epa, 15; Shutterstock Images: Dean Drobot, 13, Photo Works, 17

Design Elements
Shutterstock: GraphicDealer

Quote Source
p. 19, "Before Reaching the Majors, Some Orioles had to Work Odd Jobs to Make Ends Meet." *The Baltimore Sun.* March 7, 2015. www.baltimoresun.com.

Printed in the United States 6589

TABLE OF

CONTENTS

PLAY BALL! 4

WORKING THEIR WAY UP. 6

STAYING FIT DURING THE SEASON 10

BALLPLAYERS' WORKOUTS. . . 12

OFF-SEASON TRAINING. 16

OFF-SEASON JOBS 18

PLAYER CONTRACTS 20

ENDORSEMENTS. 22

IN THE SPOTLIGHT. 24

SUPERSTITIONS 26

RAISING MONEY TO HELP OTHERS 28

GLOSSARY 30

READ MORE 31

INTERNET SITES 31

INDEX 32

PLAY BALL!

Mike Trout of the Los Angeles Angels steps into the batter's box. He adjusts his feet to get into position. Then he stares down the pitcher. The pitcher begins his windup while Trout reads the coming pitch. The ball heads toward the plate. Trout swings hard. He crushes the ball to deep center field.

Before Trout ever steps into the batter's box, he goes through a lot of work and preparation. He watches film of the pitcher he will face. He spends hours before the game working on his swing in batting practice. He pays attention to what he's eating to make sure he's at peak physical condition heading into the game.

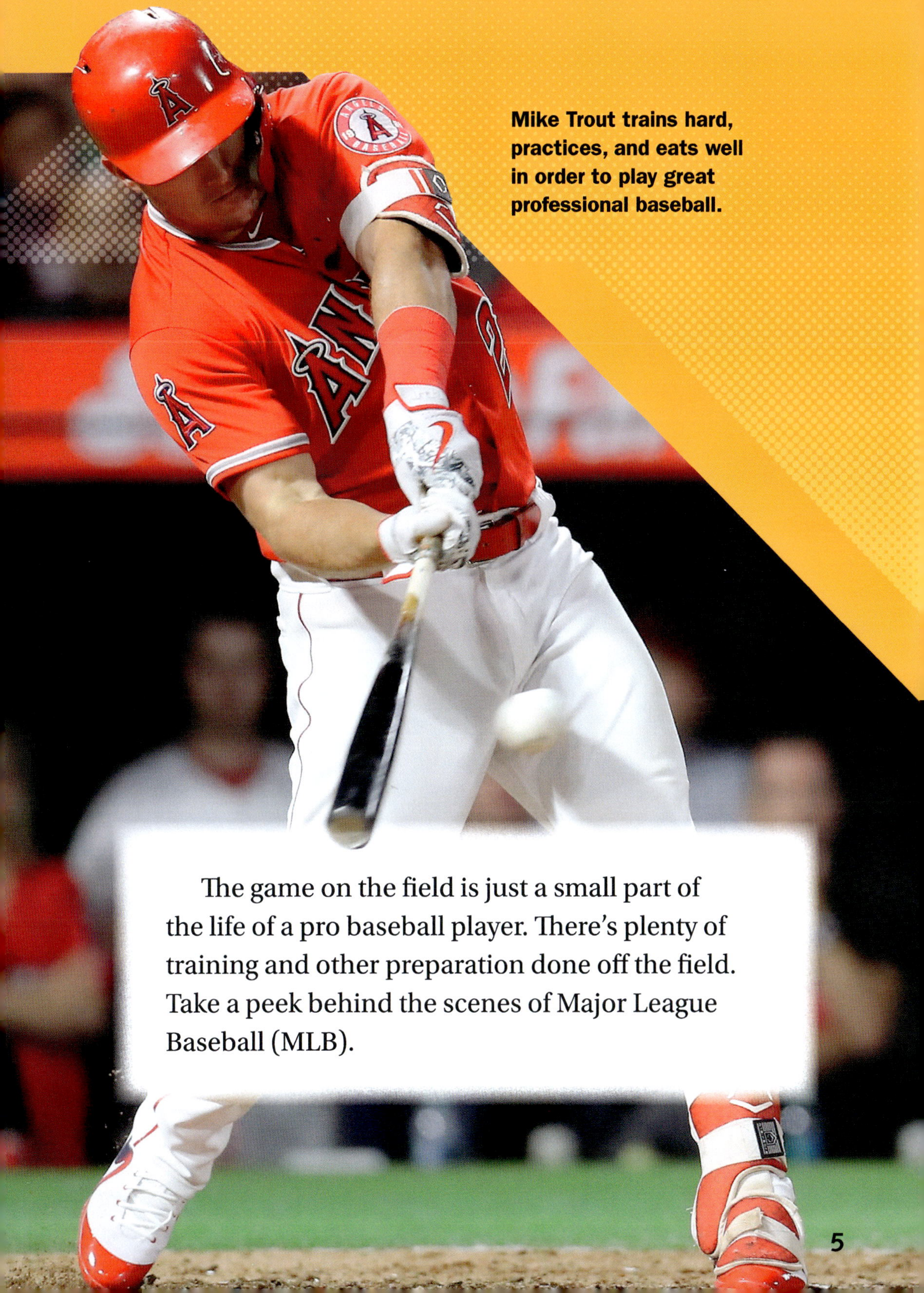

Mike Trout trains hard, practices, and eats well in order to play great professional baseball.

The game on the field is just a small part of the life of a pro baseball player. There's plenty of training and other preparation done off the field. Take a peek behind the scenes of Major League Baseball (MLB).

WORKING THEIR WAY UP

The first step for players is getting **drafted** by a team. But then they still have a long journey to the major leagues. Players have to work their way through the minor leagues. Even if a player is drafted in an early round, that doesn't mean he'll make it to the major leagues.

For Chicago Cubs standout infielder Javier Baez, the journey to the major leagues started when he was drafted as an 18-year-old. The Cubs drafted Baez with the ninth pick of the first round in 2011. They thought he had a chance to become an MLB star. But first, Baez had to prove himself in the minor leagues. He steadily worked his way through Chicago's minor-league system. He was known for his strong hitting.

draft—to choose a person to join a sports organization or team

Even stars like Chicago Cubs infielder Javier Baez have to work their way up to the major leagues.

Baez continued to move up until he was brought up to the Cubs' major-league team in 2014. Baez played less than three full seasons in the minors. Many players take much longer to reach the big leagues.

THE LEVELS OF MINOR LEAGUES

Rookie, Rookie advanced, and Class-A short season are where most players begin their careers. Seasons are usually 70 to 80 games long.

- Class A, or Low-A, has 140-game seasons.
- Class-A advanced, or High-A, is a full level above Class A. Usually only first-round draft picks start here.
- Double-A is another step up from High-A. It features a mix of young players and players who have been in the minor leagues for a while.
- Triple-A is the highest level. It is usually a player's last stop before being called up to the major leagues.

Minor-league outfielder Chevy Clark takes a taxi to meet his new team.

Most newly drafted players start in rookie ball. Approximately 15 percent of players make it to the major leagues within three years of being drafted. For most players, it takes four to six years to make it to the major leagues. After seven years, approximately two-thirds of players drafted in the first round will have reached the major leagues. But if a player has not made it by then, it's unlikely he will ever get that call.

Baltimore Orioles catcher Caleb Joseph spent six years in the minor leagues. Joseph wondered if he would ever get a shot at the majors. He almost quit baseball. But Joseph stuck with it.

Joseph finally got his chance on May 7, 2014. The Orioles called him up to play catcher after another player was injured. But making the majors doesn't always mean staying there. Joseph has spent time in both the major leagues and the minor leagues since he was called up in 2014.

FAST FACT

Rookie-league and Low-A players who are away from home for the first time often stay with host families.

STAYING FIT
DURING THE SEASON

Baseball players have different body types. Some are very lean. These players are often fast and are good at stealing bases. Other players are bulkier. They may be power hitters. But no matter their body type or fitness level, most players struggle to maintain their weight through the long 162-game season.

The season starts in February with spring training, and it can run into late October. By the end of the summer, many players have lost a lot of weight. They have to take care of their bodies throughout the season. Proper diet, workouts, sleep, and ice baths are all part of a rigorous plan to keep their bodies in shape.

Baseball players come in many shapes and sizes, but they all have to know how to take care of their bodies during the season.

KEEPING WEIGHT ON

Former major league first baseman Adam LaRoche took medication for attention deficit disorder (ADD) that caused him to lose weight. He lost more weight when he played in hot weather. Then when he got the flu in 2014, he dropped even more weight. To get back to normal weight, LaRoche drank protein shakes and ate peanut butter before going to bed.

protein—a substance found in all living plant and animal cells; foods such as meat, cheese, eggs, beans, and fish are sources of dietary protein

BALLPLAYERS' WORKOUTS

Creativity is important when working out. Players need new challenges. Center fielder Mike Trout tested himself by pushing a tractor tire. By itself, a tractor tire can weigh up to 150 pounds (68 kilograms). Trout added 310 pounds (140 kg) of weights to the tire. Then he pushed it back and forth on 25 yards (23 meters) of turf. This helped work Trout's legs and core muscles.

New York Yankees outfielder Giancarlo Stanton says yoga keeps him flexible and helps prevent injuries. He even does yoga during games. By stretching in the dugout or in the outfield, Stanton keeps his muscles warm and loose.

Box jumps are popular with athletes because they help work the leg muscles.

Box jumps are part of workouts for many players, including Washington Nationals right fielder Bryce Harper and Cincinnati Reds pitcher Michael Lorenzen. Box jumps work out the lower body. They can help increase a player's vertical leap. By landing higher on a box instead of back on the ground, the shock of landing is much easier on the knees and ankles.

Bryce Harper is a five-time All-Star and was the 2015 National League Most Valuable Player. Routine and discipline are important to Harper. He knows what his body needs to play well.

10:15 p.m.—As soon as a game ends, Harper begins preparing for the next one. After talking to the media, he eats a healthy dinner.

11 p.m.—Harper gets a massage. He then runs to help keep his legs from getting sore. He plunges into a cold tub and then heats up in a hot tub. He does this to reduce **inflammation** in his muscles and speed up **recovery**.

1 a.m.—Harper gets at least 10 hours of rest.

Noon—For breakfast, Harper likes to eat avocado on gluten-free bread, three sweet potato pancakes with chocolate chips, turkey sausage, turkey bacon, and two whole eggs mixed with two egg whites.

2 p.m.—Harper arrives at the ballpark. He does a workout. Then he gets into cold and hot tubs.

inflammation—redness, swelling, heat, and pain, usually caused by an infection or injury
recovery—the process of returning to health from sickness or injury

3 p.m.—Harper takes batting practice in the batting cage, and he hits on the field. For lunch, he eats a meal with protein, **carbohydrates**, and vegetables.

4:30 p.m.—Harper stretches and runs to loosen up. Then he works on throwing and catching.

5:15 p.m.—Harper spends time in the clubhouse playing video games. He eats a light pregame snack such as a grilled chicken salad. He drinks lots of water.

6:15 p.m.—Harper stretches, puts on his uniform, and goes to the sauna to relax.

6:45 p.m.—Harper runs sprints on the field. He mentally prepares for the game by getting some quiet time. Then it's time to play ball!

carbohydrate—a substance found in foods such as bread, rice, cereal, and potatoes that gives you energy

OFF-SEASON TRAINING

Baseball is physically challenging. Players need to run, jump, throw, and slide. Batters swing at balls traveling more than 100 miles (160 kilometers) per hour. Ballplayers need to have quick reflexes and strong, flexible muscles. They need to be well conditioned too. To get in top shape, they train during the off-season as well as during the season.

Matt Kemp, an outfielder for the Los Angeles Dodgers, had gained weight since his days as an All-Star. He wanted to lose weight to get faster.

FAST FACT

Bryce Harper put on 15 pounds (6.8 kg) of muscle before the 2017 season to help with his batting.

By slimming down and targeting his workout, Matt Kemp (right) got a lot faster.

During the 2017 off-season Kemp's workout focused on diet and fitness. He stopped eating junk food. He avoided bread and sugars. Instead, he ate more protein and vegetables. He worked to improve his core muscles, including his obliques, upper abs, lower abs, and back. He also did push-ups and pull-ups, using his own body weight as resistance. This kept him from bulking up and helped him stay flexible.

In 2017 Kemp could sprint 24.9 feet (7.5 meters) per second. His training helped him hit 26.6 feet (8.1 m) per second in 2018. His increased speed helped him run the bases and reach balls in the outfield.

OFF-SEASON JOBS

Starting salaries for minor-league players are low. They aren't paid for spring training, either. Many minor-league players have full-time jobs during the off-season. Some have more than one off-season job. Players' pay goes up as they are promoted through the minor leagues, but even at Triple-A some players keep extra jobs.

Houston Astros pitcher Collin McHugh worked for a fundraising organization during his four minor-league off-seasons. Four days a week, he worked in an office making reports and mailing envelopes. The job allowed him to fit in his workouts.

FAST FACT

Before the 1970s, most major-league players had off-season jobs too.

In the minor leagues, players often have to travel in cramped buses.

Players often rent apartments together to save money. Atlanta Braves infielder Ryan Flaherty lived in a two-bedroom apartment with five other teammates for the Chicago Cubs' Class-A team. "We had three blowup mattresses in the living room," Flaherty said. "There's so much stuff that people don't see off the field."

Players usually keep living with several roommates and working other jobs until they make the major leagues. At that point, they get a huge pay increase. But Detroit Tigers pitcher Michael Fulmer hasn't quit the job he held when he was in the minors. In the off-season, the American League Rookie of the Year works as a plumber's assistant.

PLAYER CONTRACTS

A player signs a contract when he joins a team. A player's agent works for the player to make sure he gets the best contract possible. An agent has specialized experience in sports contracts. The agent **negotiates** terms of the contract with the team. The agent also negotiates the player's salary and other benefits. These benefits include the length of the contract and performance bonuses. Agents earn money based on the contracts they negotiate.

If a player's contract ends and he has spent at least six years in the major leagues, he can become a free agent. He is free to sign with any team that offers him a contract. One part of an agent's job is helping his players find teams that will give them good deals when they are free agents.

negotiate—to bargain or discuss something to come to an agreement

Agent Scott Boras (right) negotiated a contract for his client, Royce Lewis (center), with the Minnesota Twins.

FAST FACT

Some minor-league players get bats and gloves from their agents. Otherwise, the players must purchase the equipment themselves.

ENDORSEMENTS

A player's agent does more than negotiate salaries. Agents also work to get players **endorsements** and set up public appearances. They work to promote the baseball player's image, abilities, and career.

A major-league player can earn a lot of money outside of his baseball contract. Star players endorse gloves, bats, cleats, and other gear. They can also endorse items beyond baseball, such as cereal, soda, and clothing.

Baseball players often use the products they endorse. For example, if a player endorses Nike, he will likely wear Nike cleats and batting gloves. Players often receive this equipment as part of their endorsement deal. If they endorse a clothing brand, they will often wear that brand too.

endorsement—a statement or advertisement in support of a product or service

Los Angeles Angels first baseman Albert Pujols endorses a wide range of products from baseball gear to cereal.

IN THE SPOTLIGHT

Players must be good role models. If they aren't, players may find it hard to keep their jobs. Teams want players to be popular with fans, and they expect players to connect with the fan base. Players need to show good sportsmanship on the field and be polite when talking with fans or others away from the field.

Before and after games, players are interviewed in their locker rooms by the media. They might not always want to do it, especially after a tough loss. But teams encourage their players to cooperate with the media. They know it's an important part of their outreach to fans.

FAST FACT

Social media sites such as Twitter and Instagram have increased players' visibility to fans. Players can instantly share their thoughts and photos with their followers.

Cincinnati Reds third baseman Eugenio Suarez (right) does a post-game interview.

Promotional events are a good chance for players to connect with people and fans in their local communities. These events often promote the team or a product. After winning the 2017 World Series, the Houston Astros held promotional events for fans. Fans got a special opportunity to talk with players. Players signed special-edition baseball cards provided at the event.

SUPERSTITIONS

Players often try to do the same thing before or during each game. Consistency and preparation are important in baseball. Having a routine can help a player mentally prepare for a game. These preparations often turn into **superstitions**. Many players believe these superstitions will help them be successful in games. Other times they believe certain behaviors will bring them bad luck.

Former outfielder Richie Ashburn would take his bat home with him when he was on a hot streak. Ashburn thought the bat was lucky and didn't trust the clubhouse staff to give him the same bat the next day.

FAST FACT

Some players won't talk to a pitcher during the game if he hasn't allowed a hit. They believe if they do, they could jinx the pitcher's success.

superstition—a belief that an action can affect the outcome of a future event

Washington Nationals pitcher Brandon Kintzler wears a rally cap. The rally cap is worn when a team is down and needs to come back to win.

Some superstitions seem to have nothing to do with baseball. Justin Verlander used to eat tacos before every game because he thought they helped him pitch better. After a bad season, he quit the ritual.

Raising Money to Help Others

Baseball players use their fame to help others. They ask for donations for worthy causes. Many support their favorite **charities**. Others create their own charities.

When a tornado hit his hometown of Tuscaloosa, Alabama, in 2011, pitcher David Robertson wanted to help. Robertson is known for cuffing his pants at the knee to show his high socks. So he founded High Socks for Hope to help people recover. Robertson pledged $100 to his foundation for every batter he struck out and $200 for every game he saved. After Hurricane Harvey hit Houston, Texas, in 2017, the foundation gave away more than 1,000 pieces of furniture, mattresses, and household items to people affected by the disaster.

charity—an organization that raises money and provides help to those in need

Derek Jeter still helps children with his Turn 2 charity even though he has retired.

Former Red Sox slugger David Ortiz started a charity to help kids in his home country of the Dominican Republic and in Boston, Massachusetts, where he played. This charity helps cover the costs of children's heart surgeries for low-income families. Ortiz still runs the organization.

FAST FACT

Major League Baseball partners with many nonprofit organizations to support worthy causes, including Make-A-Wish Foundation, Susan G. Komen, and Boys & Girls Club of America.

GLOSSARY

carbohydrate (kar-boh-HYE-drate)—a substance found in foods such as bread, rice, cereal, and potatoes that gives you energy

charity (CHAYR-uh-tee)—an organization that raises money and provides help to those in need

draft (DRAFT)—to choose a person to join a sports organization or team

endorsement (in-DORS-muhnt)—a statement or advertisement in support of a product or service

inflammation (in-fluh-MAY-shuhn)—redness, swelling, heat, and pain, usually caused by an infection or injury

negotiate (ni-GOH-shee-ate)—to bargain or discuss something to come to an agreement

protein (PROH-teen)—a substance found in all living plant and animal cells; foods such as meat, cheese, eggs, beans, and fish are sources of dietary protein

recovery (ri-KOV-ur-ree)—the process of returning to health from sickness or injury

superstition (soo-pur-STI-shuhn)—a belief that an action can affect the outcome of a future event

READ MORE

Braun, Eric. *Baseball Is a Numbers Game: A Fan's Guide to Stats.* Know the Stats. North Mankato, Minn.: Capstone, 2018.

Hetrick, Hans. *Baseball's Record Breakers.* Record Breakers. North Mankato, Minn.: Capstone, 2017.

Kramer, S. A. *Baseball's Greatest Hitters: From Ty Cobb to Miguel Cabrera*. Step into Reading. New York: Random House, 2016.

INTERNET SITES

Use FactHound to find Internet sites related to this book.

Visit www.facthound.com

Just type in 9781543554274 and go.

INDEX

agents, 20, 21, 22
Ashburn, Richie, 26

Baez, Javier, 6–7

contracts, 20, 22

endorsements, 22

Flaherty, Ryan, 19
free agents, 20
Fulmer, Michael, 19

Harper, Bryce, 13–15, 17
High Socks for Hope, 28
Hurricane Harvey, 28

Joseph, Caleb, 9

Kemp, Matt, 16–17

LaRoche, Adam, 11
Lorenzen, Michael, 13

McHugh, Collin, 18
minor leagues, 6–9, 18–19, 21

Ortiz, David, 29

Robertson, David, 28

Stanton, Giancarlo, 12
superstitions, 26–27

Trout, Mike, 4, 12

Verlander, Justin, 27

World Series, 25